P9-DTN-418

Whales

Kate Riggs

seedlings

CREATIVE EDUCATION • CREATIVE PAPERBACKS

Published by Creative Education and Creative Paperbacks
P.O. Box 227, Mankato, Minnesota 56002
Creative Education and Creative Paperbacks are
imprints of The Creative Company
www.thecreativecompany.us

Design by Ellen Huber
Production by Chelsey Luther
Printed in the United States of America

Photographs by Corbis (John Hyde/AlaskaStock, Hiroya
Minakuchi/Minden Pictures, Mike Parry/Minden Pictures,
Denis Scott, Paul Souders, Christopher Swann/Science Photo
Library, Jody Watt/Design Pics), Dreamstime (Boppintheblues,
Ken Moore, Joanne Weston), Shutterstock (leonello calvetti,
CampCrazy Photography, Miles Away Photography, Jay
Ondreicka, Eduardo Rivero, Michael Rosskothen, TsuneoMP),
SuperStock (Minden Pictures, Pacific Stock-Design Pics, Stock
Connection)

Library of Congress Cataloging-in-Publication Data
Riggs, Kate.
Whales / Kate Riggs.
p. cm. — (Seedlings)
Summary: A kindergarten-level introduction to whales,
covering their growth process, behaviors, the oceans they call
home, and such defining features as their blowholes.
Includes index.
ISBN 978-1-60818-517-7 (hardcover)
ISBN 978-1-62832-117-3 (pbk)
1. Whales—Juvenile literature. I. Title. II. Series: Seedlings.

QL737.C4R543 2015
599.5—dc23   2014000189

CCSS: RI.K.1, 2, 3, 4, 5, 6, 7;
RI.1.1, 2, 3, 4, 5, 6, 7; RF.K.1, 3; RF.1.1

First Edition
9 8 7 6 5 4 3 2 1

TABLE OF CONTENTS

Hello, whales!

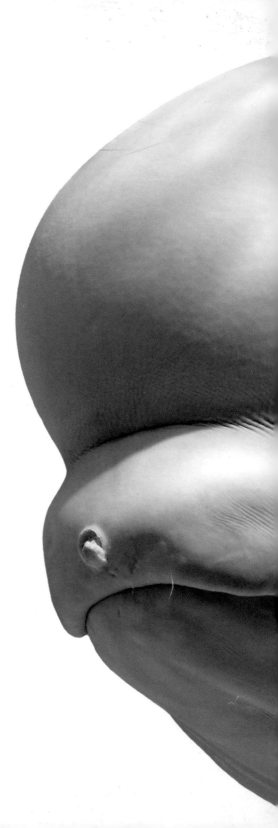

Whales live in the oceans.

There are 38 kinds of whales.

Whales have long bodies with tails. Most whales are dark colors. Beluga whales are white.

Some whales have teeth.

Other whales have baleen.

All whales breathe through blowholes on their heads.

Whales eat fish and other animals. Baleen whales catch tiny animals in their baleen.

A calf is a baby whale.

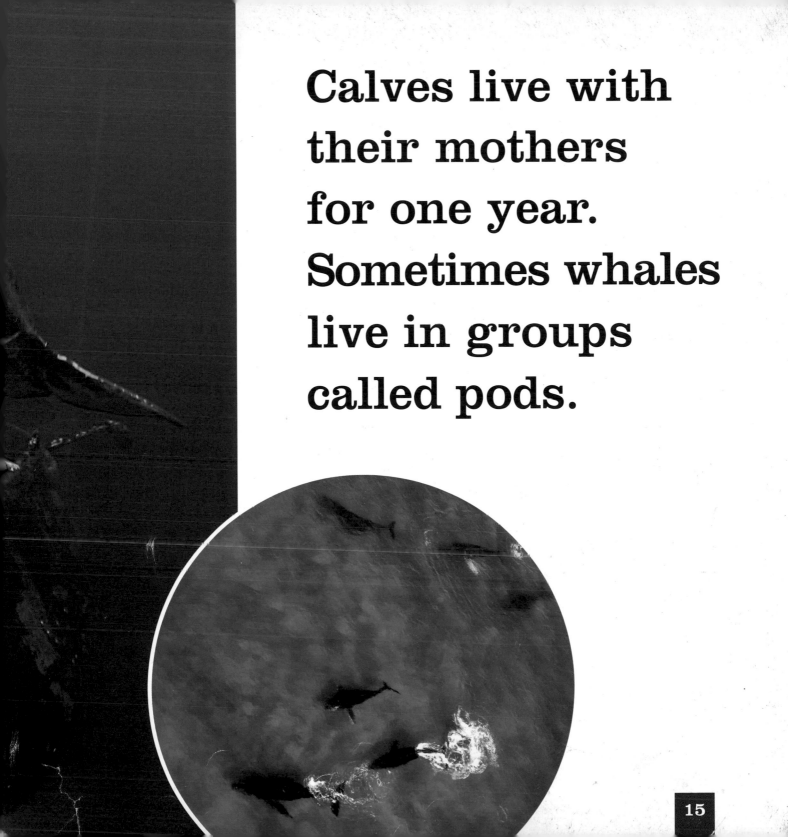

Calves live with
their mothers
for one year.
Sometimes whales
live in groups
called pods.

Whales swim all day.

They jump out of the water and splash down!

Goodbye, whales!

Picture a Whale

teeth

skin

tail

fin

eye

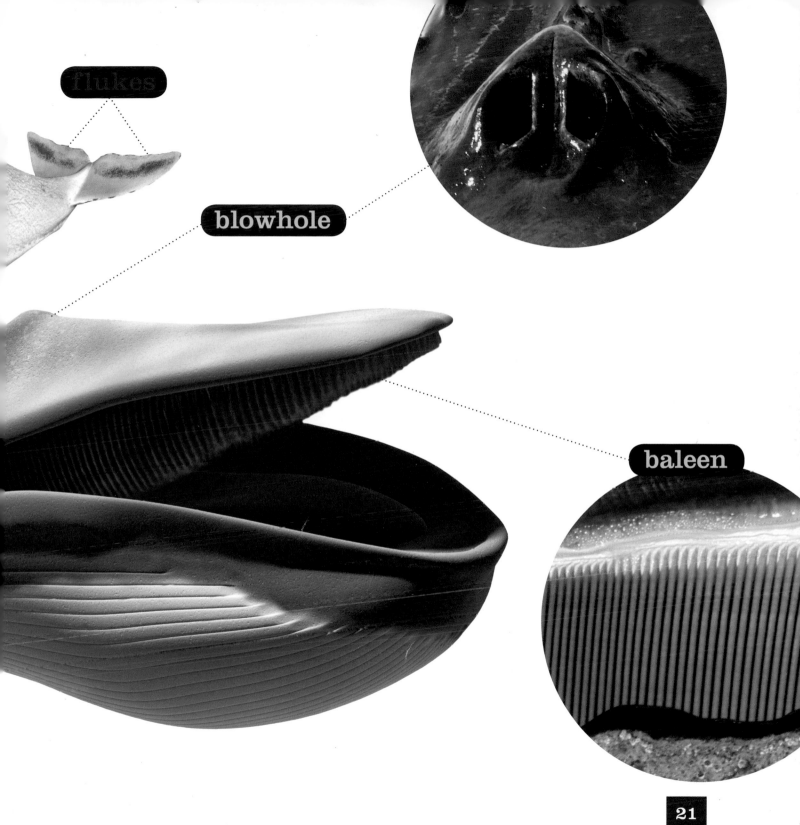

flukes

blowhole

baleen

Words to Know

baleen: a bony, comb-like feeding system inside the mouth of some whales

oceans: big areas of deep, salty water

Read More

Herriges, Ann. *Whales*.
Minneapolis: Bellwether Media, 2007.

Turnbull, Stephanie. *Whale*.
North Mankato, Minn.: Smart Apple Media, 2013.

Websites

Blue Whales
http://video.nationalgeographic.com/video/whale_bluecalls
Learn more about blue whales, and listen to their sounds.

Whale Activities
http://www.enchantedlearning.com/themes/whale.shtml
Keep learning about whales, with the help of fun activities.

Index